constitution
of the
islamic republic
of iran

Distributed by:
ISLAMIC PUBLIC RELATIONS
P.O. Box 3095
New York, N.Y. 10008 USA

CONSTITUTION OF
THE ISLAMIC REPUBLIC
OF IRAN

Translated from the Persian
by
HAMID ALGAR

MIZAN PRESS
Berkeley

The device on the cover is the official emblem of the Islamic Republic of Iran, adopted in May 1980 in accordance with Article 18 of the Constitution. It is a stylized presentation of the first part of the Islamic profession of faith, *"La ilaha illa 'Llah* (There is no god but God)." The emblem is particularly appropriate given the fact that *tauhid,* the principle of divine unity, is to underlie the new order in Iran.

Copyright © 1980 by Mizan Press
All Rights Reserved
Designed by Adolfo Castillo

Library of Congress Cataloging in Publication Data

Iran. Constitution, 1979. English.
    Constitution of the Islamic Republic of Iran.

    1. Iran—Constitutional law. I. Algar, Hamid. II. Title.
Law   342.55'023   80-19896
ISBN 0-933782-07-1 hard cover
ISBN 0-933782-02-0 paperback

10 9 8 7 6 5 4 3 2 1

Manufactured in the United States of America

Contents

Preface

Constitutionalism has a long history in Iran. Interest in establishing a constitutional form of government, spurred partly by the influence of Western models and partly by developments in neighboring Turkey, first appeared in the last decade of the nineteenth century. The constitutional limitation of monarchical power was the principal goal of the revolutionary movement of 1905-1909. This movement, directed chiefly by the major religious leaders of the day, brought about the capitulation of Muzaffar ud-Din Shah in the summer of 1906, and the first *Majlis* in Iranian history prepared a constitution, consisting of a preamble and 51 articles, which was ratified on December 30, 1906. To it were added 107 supplementary articles, ratified on October 7, 1907. The constitution was amended four times, in accordance with the dictates of the Pahlavi family, in 1925, 1949, 1957, and 1967.

Theoretically, the constitution of 1906, with its later supplements and amendments, remained in force until the triumph of the Islamic Revolution in February 1979. In fact, however, it was almost always a dead letter: successive Shahs, with their obduracy powerfully reinforced by a succession of foreign patrons—Russian, British, and American—were able to maintain the reality of absolutism behind a facade of constitutional forms. Sayyid Hasan Mudarris, in the 1920's, and Abul-Qasim Kashani and Dr. Musaddiq, in the 1940's, strove unsuccessfully to obtain true implementation of the constitution. Only toward the end of his inauspicious rule did the recently deceased Shah take some interest in the constitution. This sudden interest in constitutional monarchy, a ploy intended to check the Revolution, led to such improbable spectacles as Ardeshir Zahedi, the Shah's envoy in Washington, pontificating on the need for respecting the constitution.

With the ineluctable advance of the Revolution toward victory, it became plain that a totally new constitution would be required in the new Islamic order. It was not merely that the 1906 constitution had always been flouted, or even that it provided for the institution of monarchy, which was now to be abolished. It was an anachronism, reflecting the needs and aspirations of another age, and based largely upon foreign, and especially Belgian, models. The Islamic Revolution of 1978-1979 was characterized by a far greater degree of ideological clarity and consciousness than the Constitutional Revolution; a constitution that was wholly and distinctively Islamic was bound to emerge from it.

Accordingly, Imam Khomeini, in his declaration of January 12, 1979 announcing the formation of the Council of the Islamic Revolution, declared one of the tasks of the transitional revolutionary government to be "the formation of a constituent assembly (*majlis-i mu'assisan*) composed of the elected representatives of the people in order to approve the new constitution of the Islamic Republic." A draft constitution, in 151 articles, was drawn up and published in June.[1] It became the subject of a wide-ranging public debate, reflected in the lively and variegated press that came into being in Iran after the revolution. Suggestions for changes and additions were also received from Muslim individuals and organizations outside Iran, so that the debate became a kind of informal consultation among Muslims for the production of a constitution that might have wider applicability than in Iran alone.

Meanwhile, in order to facilitate the swift amendment of the draft constitution and to move forward rapidly with the construction of new political institutions, it was decided to replace the broad constituent assembly originally proposed by Imam Khomeini with an Assembly of Experts (*Majlis-i Khubragan*). Elections for this Assembly took place on August 3 throughout the country, although returns for several areas were delayed because voters were harassed by various counterrevolutionary forces. The Assembly convened in Tehran, in the building of the former Iranian Senate, and subjected the draft constitution to minute examination and extensive revision. Proceedings of the Assembly were broadcast over Iranian television and edited transcripts appeared daily in the press. Barely a single article passed without extensive discussion of both substance and wording. The debates that took place constitute an important chapter not only in the history of the Iranian revolution but also in the evolution of contemporary Islamic political thought.[2]

---

[1] The English translation was published as a supplement to *Iran Voice*, Bulletin of the Iranian Embassy in Washington.

[2] Dr. Ali Ghaffuri, a member of the Assembly of Experts, informed me in Tehran in late December 1979 that he was preparing a full history of its work, complete with an analysis of the differing points of view represented.

The text that received final approval from the Assembly of Experts when work was completed in November differed considerably from the draft in bulk, structure, and content. The most important single difference was the introduction into the constitution of the key concept of *vilayat-i faqih,* "the governance of the *faqih*." This doctrine, which Imam Khomeini had outlined at length in his celebrated lectures at Najaf in 1969, is the keystone of the new political structure, ensuring that the Republic will be Islamic in substance and daily functioning as well as designation.[3] It is true that Article Two of the supplementary laws of 1907 had provided for a committee of five high-ranking scholars to ensure that no legislation passed by the *Majlis* would be contrary to Islam, but the article was never implemented. We may be certain that, in keeping with the character of the Islamic Revolution, the principle of *vilayat-i faqih* will be fully implemented in the manner laid down in the new Constitution.

The Constitution was approved in a referendum held throughout Iran on December 2-3. It already appears likely that a number of amendments will prove necessary, but the Constitution of the Islamic Republic of Iran is a remarkable document as it stands, a product of the only Islamic revolutionary movement of modern times and one of the major accomplishments of the new Islamic order in the first year of its existence.

Hamid Algar

Berkeley
Ramadhan 1400 / Mordad 1359 / July 1980

---

[3] For an annotated translation of these lectures, see *Islam and Revolution: Writings and Declarations of Imam Khomeini* (Berkeley: Mizan Press), forthcoming.

CONSTITUTION OF THE ISLAMIC REPUBLIC OF IRAN

IN THE NAME OF GOD, THE COMPASSIONATE, THE MERCIFUL

Verily We sent Our Messengers with clear signs and sent down with them the Book and the Balance in order that men might act in equity.

Qur'an, 57:25

Introduction

The Constitution of the Islamic Republic of Iran sets forth the cultural, social, political, and economic foundations of Iranian society on the basis of the Islamic principles and norms that represent the heartfelt desire of the Islamic nation. This basic desire was determined by the very nature of the great Islamic Revolution of Iran, as well as the course of the Muslim people's struggle, from its beginning until victory—as reflected in the decisive and forceful slogans used by all segments of the population. At this time, too, in the dawn of their great victory, our people are striving with all of their being to attain their final goal.

The basic characteristic of the Revolution, which distinguishes it from other movements that have taken place in Iran during the past hundred years, is its ideological and Islamic nature. After experiencing the anti-despotic constitutional movement and the anti-imperialist movement centered on the nationalization of the oil industry, the Muslim people of Iran learned the valuable lesson that the obvious and fundamental reason for the failure of those movements was their lack of an ideological basis. It is well known that the intellectual line of Islam and the direction provided by militant religious leaders played an essential role in various recent movements. Nonetheless, because the struggles waged in the course of those movements departed from the true positions of Islam, they quickly fell into stagnation. Thus it was that the awakened conscience of the nation, under the leadership of that precious *marja'-i taqlid*, Ayatullah al-Uzma Imam Khomeini, came to perceive the necessity of pursuing an authentically Islamic and ideological line in its struggles. The militant religious leaders of the country, who had always been in the forefront of popular movements, together with the committed writers and intellectuals bestirred themselves anew as a result of his leadership, so that the beginning of the most recent movement of the Iranian people is to be put at 1382 of the lunar Islamic calendar, corresponding to 1341 of the solar Islamic calendar [1962 of the Christian calendar].

The Dawn of the Movement

The devastating protest of Imam Khomeini against the American conspiracy known as the "White Revolution," which was a step intended to strengthen the bases of despotic government and reinforce the political, cultural, and economic dependence of Iran on world imperialism, brought into being a united movement of the Iranian people and, immediately afterwards, a momentous revolution of the Muslim nation in the month of Khordad, 1342 [June 1963]. Although this revolution was drowned in a blood bath, it was in reality a new point of departure. A glorious movement of massive revolt now began to blossom around the central figure of the Imam, incorporating the Islamic leadership and confirmed and reinforced by the uprising. Despite his exile from Iran after his protest against the shameful law on capitulations, which provided legal immunity for American advisers, the firm bond between the Imam and the nation persisted, and the Muslim people, particularly committed intellectuals and militant religious leaders, continued their struggle in the face of banishment and imprisonment, torture and execution.

Throughout this time, the conscious and responsible segment of society was bringing enlightenment to the people from the strongholds provided by the mosque, the religious teaching institution, and the university; drawing inspiration from the fruitful and revolutionary teachings of Islam, they began steadfast and positive efforts to raise the level of the Muslim people's awareness of revolution and ideology. At first the despotic regime attempted to suppress the Islamic movement with barbaric attacks on the Fayziya madrasa, [Tehran] University, and all other active centers of revolution. Then, in an effort to escape the revolutionary anger of the people, it had recourse to the most savage and brutal methods; execution by firing squad, the endurance of medieval tortures, and long terms of imprisonment were the price our Muslim nation had to pay to prove its firm determination to continue the struggle. The Islamic Revolution of Iran was nurtured by the blood of hundreds of young believers, women and men, who met the firing squads at dawn with cries of *"Allahu akbar,"* or who were gunned down by the enemy in streets and marketplaces. Meanwhile, the continuing declarations and messages from the Imam that were issued on various occasions extended and deepened the consciousness and determination of the Muslim nation to the utmost.

Islamic Government

The plan of Islamic government, based upon the governance of the *faqih*, as set forth by Imam Khomeīni at the height of the period of repression and strangulation practiced by the despotic regime, created a new, distinct, and consistent motive for the people, opening up before them the authentic path of Islamic ideological struggle. This in turn caused militant and committed Muslims to intensify their struggle both within the country and abroad.

The movement continued on this course until finally the dissatisfaction and intense anger of the people shook the foundations of the regime violently. This came about because of the constantly increasing repression practiced by the regime at home, and the reflection of the struggle at the international level after exposure of the regime by religious leaders and militant students. The regime and its masters were compelled to decrease the intensity of repression and to "liberalize" the political atmosphere of the country. Their intention was to open a safety valve, which they hoped would prevent their eventual downfall. But the people—aroused, conscious, and determined to follow the decisive and unerring leadership of the Imam—embarked on a comprehensive, all-embracing, unified, and triumphant uprising.

The Anger of the People

The publication of an article insulting the honor of the religious leadership and Imam Khomeini in particular on Day 17, 1356 [January 7, 1978] quickened the revolutionary movement and caused an outburst of popular anger across the country. The regime attempted to quell the volcano of the people's anger by drowning the uprising in blood, but the bloodshed only stepped up the pulse rate of the Revolution. Commemorations of the martyrs of the Revolution, on the seventh and fortieth days after their death, like a series of steady heartbeats brought greater life, ardor, and enthusiasm to this movement, which now was unfolding across the country. People working in all government establishments took an active part by mounting a general strike and participating in street demonstrations to overthrow the tyrannical regime. The widespread solidarity between men and women of all segments of society, belonging to both the religious and the political wings of the movement, played a clearly influential role in the struggle. Women were actively and massively present in a most obvious manner in all stages of this great struggle. The common sight of mothers with infants in their arms running toward the scene of battle and the barrels of machineguns demonstrated the essential and decisive role played by this major segment of society in the struggle.

The Price Paid by the People

After slightly more than a year of continuous and steadfast struggle, this sapling of a revolution, watered by the blood of 60,000 martyrs and 100,000 wounded and disabled, not to mention billions of tumans' worth of property damage, came to bear fruit amidst loud cries of "Independence! Freedom! Islamic government!" This great movement, which had attained victory through reliance upon faith, unity, and the decisiveness of its leadership at every critical and sensitive juncture, as well as the self-sacrificing spirit of the people, succeeded in upsetting all the calculations of imperialism and destroying all its institutions, thereby opening a new chapter in the history of mass popular revolutions throughout the world.

Bahman 21 and 22, 1357 [February 12 and 13, 1979] witnessed the collapse of the monarchical regime, and domestic tyranny and foreign domination, both of which were based upon it, were shattered. With this great victory, the vanguard of Islamic government, the longstanding wish and desire of the Muslim people, gave the glad tidings of final victory.

Unanimously, and with the participation of the *maraji'-i taqlid*, the scholars of Islam, and the leadership, the Iranian people declared their final and firm decision, in the referendum on the Islamic Republic, to bring about a new political system, that of the Islamic Republic. A 98.2% majority of the people voted for this system.

The Constitution of the Islamic Republic of Iran, setting forth as it does the political, social, cultural, and economic institutions and relations that are to exist in our society, must now provide for the strengthening of the bases of Islamic government, and make manifest the new model of government that is to be erected on the ruins of the previous despotic regime.

The Form of Government in Islam

In the view of Islam, government does not derive from the interests of a certain class, nor does it serve the domination of an individual or a group. It represents rather the crystallization of the political ideal of a people who bear a common faith and common outlook, taking an organized form in order to aid the process of intellectual and ideological evolution toward the final goal, i.e., movement toward God. In the course of its revolutionary development, our nation has cleansed itself of the dust and impurities that accumulated during the tyrannical regime and purged itself of foreign ideological influences, returning to the intellectual positions and authentic world-view of Islam. It now intends to establish an ideal and model society on the basis of Islamic criteria. The mission of the Constitution is to give objective existence to the credal bases of the movement and to create conditions under which man may be nurtured by the noble and universal values of Islam.

With regard to the Islamic content of the Iranian Revolution, which has been a movement aimed at the triumph of all oppressed and deprived persons over their oppressors, the Constitution provides the necessary basis for ensuring the continuation of the Revolution at home and abroad. In particular, in the development of external relations, the Revolution will strive, in concert with other Islamic and popular movements, to prepare the way for the formation of a single world community, in accordance with the Qur'anic verse *"This your nation is a single nation, and I am your Lord, so worship Me"* (21:92), and to assure the continuation of the struggle for the liberation of all deprived and oppressed peoples in the world.

With regard to the essential character of this great movement, the Constitution guarantees the rejection of all forms of intellectual and social tyranny and economic monopoly, and aims at entrusting the destinies of the people to the people themselves in order to break completely with the system of tyranny. This is in accordance with the Qur'anic verse *"He removes from them their burdens and the fetters that had weighed upon them"* (7:157).

In creating, on the basis of ideological outlook, the political institutions and organs that are the foundation of society, the righteous will assume the responsibility of governing and administering the country, in accordance with the Qur'anic verse *"Verily My righteous bondsmen inherit the earth"* (21:105). Legislation setting forth regulations for the administration of society will be established on the basis of the Qur'an and the Sunna. The exercise of meticulous and painstaking supervision by just, pious, and committed scholars of Islam ("just *fuqaha*") is an absolute necessity. In addition, the aim of government is to foster the growth of man in such a way that he progresses toward the establishment of a divine order, in accordance with the Qur'anic phrase *"And to God is the journeying"* (3:28), and to create favorable conditions for the emergence and blossoming of man's innate capacities so that the theomorphic dimensions of man are manifested. This is in accordance with the injunction of the Prophet, upon whom be peace, "Acquire the divine characteristics." The attainment of this goal depends on the broad and active participation of all segments of society in the process of social development.

In this respect, then, the Constitution provides the basis for such participation by all members of society in all stages of the political decision-making process on which the destiny of the country depends. In this way, during the course of human development toward perfection, each individual will himself be involved in, and responsible for, his own growth and advancement as well as the leadership of society. In precisely this lies the realization of the government of the oppressed upon earth, in accordance with the Qur'anic verse *"And we wish to show favor to those who have been oppressed upon earth, and to make of them leaders and inheritors"* (28:5).

Governance of the Just *Faqih*

In keeping with the principles of governance and the permanent necessity of leadership, the Constitution provides for the establishment of leadership by a *faqih* possessing the necessary qualifications and recognized as leader by the people. This is in accordance with the saying "The conduct of affairs is to be in the hands of those who are learned concerning God and are trustworthy guardians of that which He has permitted and that which He has forbidden." Such leadership will prevent any deviation by the various organs of government from their essential Islamic duties.

The Economy Is a Means, Not an End

In strengthening the foundations of the economy, the fundamental consideration will be satisfying the material needs of man in the course of his overall growth and development. This principle contrasts with other economic systems, where the aim is the concentration and accumulation of wealth and the maximization of profit. In materialist schools of thought, the economy represents an end in itself, so that it comes to be a subversive and corrupting factor in the course of man's development. In Islam, the economy is a means, intended only to contribute to the attainment of the ultimate goal.

The economic program of Islam consists, then, of providing the means needed for the emergence of the various creative capacities of man. It is the duty of the Islamic government to furnish all citizens with equal and suitable opportunities, to provide them with work, and to satisfy their essential needs, so that the course of their progress may be assured.

Woman in the Constitution

In the creation of Islamic social institutions, all elements of humanity that hitherto served the multifaceted foreign exploitation of our country are to regain their true identity and human rights. As a part of this process, it is only natural that women should benefit from a particularly large augmentation of their rights, because of the greater oppression that they suffered under the despotic regime.

The family is the fundamental unit of society and the major center for the growth and advancement of man. Compatibility with respect to belief and ideal is the main consideration in the establishment of a family, for the family provides the primary basis for man's development and growth. It is the duty of Islamic government to provide the necessary facilities for the attainment of this goal. This view of the family unit delivers woman from being regarded as an object or as an instrument in the service of consumerism and exploitation. Not only does woman recover thereby her momentous and precious function of motherhood, rearing alert and active human beings, she also becomes the fellow struggler of man in all the different areas of life. Given the weighty responsibilities that woman thus assumes, she is accorded in Islam great value and nobility.

An Ideological Army

In the formation and equipping of the country's defense forces, due attention must be paid to faith and ideology as the basic norms. The Army of the Islamic Republic and the Corps of Guards of the Revolution are to be organized with this in mind, and they will be responsible not only for guarding and preserving the frontiers of the country, but also for fulfilling the ideological mission of jihad in God's path; that is, extending the sovereignty of God's law throughout the world. This will be in accordance with the Qur'anic verse *"Prepare against them whatever force you are able to muster, and horses ready*

*for battle, striking fear into the enemy of God and your
enemy, and others beyond them"* (8:60).

The Judiciary in the Constitution

The judiciary represents a vital concern, given its close
connection with the preservation of the rights of the people in accordance with the line followed by the Islamic
movement, and the prevention of deviation within the
Islamic nation. Provision has therefore been made for
the creation of a judicial system based on Islamic justice
and operated by just judges who are acquainted with the
precise criteria laid down by Islam. Given the sensitive
nature of the judicial institution, and the need for assuring its full conformity to Islamic precept, it must shun
all inappropriate connections. This is in accordance with
the Qur'anic verse *"When you judge among the people,
then judge justly"* (4:58).

Executive Power

Considering the particular importance of the executive
power in implementing the laws and ordinances of Islam
for the sake of establishing society on the basis of just relations, and considering, too, its vital role in attaining
the ultimate goal of all life, the executive power must
work toward the creation of an Islamic society. The con-
striction of the executive power within complex and in-
hibiting structures that delay or impede the attainment
of this goal is rejected by Islam. The system of bureauc-
racy, the result and product of despotic forms of government, will be firmly rejected, so there can be an executive
system that functions efficiently and swiftly in the fulfillment of its administrative duties.

Mass-Communication Media

The mass-communication media, radio and television, must serve the diffusion of Islamic culture in order to aid the further development of the Islamic Revolution. To this end, there is benefit in the healthy encounter of differing viewpoints, but the media must strictly refrain from the diffusion and propagation of destructive and anti-Islamic qualities.

It is incumbent on all to adhere to the principles of this Constitution, for it regards as its highest aim the freedom and dignity of the human race and provides for the growth and advancement of man. It is also necessary that the Muslim people should participate actively in the construction of Islamic society by electing responsible, knowledgeable, and believing representatives and supervising their work. They may then hope for success in building an ideal Islamic society that can be a model for all the people of the world and a witness to them. This is in accordance with the Qur'anic verse *"Thus We made you a median nation, that you might be witnesses to men"* (2:143).

Representatives

The Assembly of Experts, composed of representatives of the people, completed its task of writing the Constitution, on the basis of the draft proposed by the government as well as all the proposals received from different groups of the people, in one hundred seventy-five articles arranged in twelve chapters, on the eve of the fifteenth century after the migration of the Noble Prophet (peace and blessings be upon him and his family), the founder of the liberating movement of Islam, and in accordance with the aims and motives set out above. It is the hope of that assembly that this century will witness the universal establishment of a government of the oppressed and the complete downfall of their oppressors.

Chapter I
General Principles

ARTICLE 1

The form of government of Iran is that of an Islamic Republic, which received an affirmative vote from the Iranian people on the basis of their longstanding belief in the Qur'anic government of truth and justice, after their victorious Islamic Revolution led by the eminent *marja'-i taqlid*, Ayatullah al-Uzma Imam Khomeini, in the referendum of Farvardin 9 and 10 in the year 1358 of the solar Islamic calendar, corresponding to Jummadi al-Ula 1 and 2 in the year 1399 of the lunar Islamic calendar [March 29 and 30, 1979].

ARTICLE 2

The Islamic Republic is a system of government based on belief in:

a.   the One God (as stated in the Islamic creed "There is no god but God"), His exclusive possession of sovereignty and the right to legislate, and the necessity of submission to His commands;

b.   divine revelation and its fundamental role in the expounding of laws;

c.   the return to God in the hereafter, and the constructive role of this belief in man's ascending progress toward God;

d.   the justice of God in creation and legislation;

e.   continuous leadership and guidance, and its fundamental role in assuring the continuity of the revolution of Islam;

f.   the exalted dignity and value of man, and his freedom, joined to responsibilities, before God;

which secures equity, justice, political, economic, social, and cultural independence, and national solidarity, by recourse to:

a.   continuous *ijtihad* of the *fuqaha* possessing the necessary qualifications, exercised on the basis of the Book of God and the Sunna of the Ma'sumin, upon all of whom be peace;

b.   recourse to arts and sciences and the most advanced results of human experience, together with the effort to carry them still farther forward;

c.   rejection of all forms of oppression, both the infliction and the endurance of it, and of dominance, both its imposition and its acceptance.

ARTICLE 3

In order to attain the objectives specified in Article 2, the government of the Islamic Republic of Iran has the duty of directing all its resources to the following goals:

a.   the creation of a favorable environment for the growth of spiritual virtues based upon faith and piety and the struggle against all forms of vice and corruption;

b. raising the level of public awareness in all areas, through the correct use of the press, the mass media, and other means;

c. free education and physical training for everyone at all levels, and the facilitation and expansion of higher education;

d. strengthening the spirit of inquiry, investigation, and initiative in all areas of science, technology, and culture, as well as Islamic studies, by establishing research centers and encouraging researchers;

e. the complete expulsion of imperialism and the prevention of foreign influence;

f. the elimination of all forms of tyranny and autocracy and all attempts to monopolize power;

g. the securing of political and social freedoms within the limits of the law;

h. ensuring the participation of the entire people in the determination of their political, economic, social, and cultural destiny;

i. the abolition of all forms of impermissible discrimination and the provision of just opportunities for all, in both material and non-material matters;

j. the creation of a proper administrative system and the elimination of unnecessary government organizations;

k. strengthening the defense of the nation to the utmost degree by means of universal military training for the sake of preserving the independence, territorial integrity, and Islamic order of the country;

l. the planning of a correct and just economic system, in accordance with Islamic criteria, in order to create prosperity, remove poverty, and abolish all forms of deprivation with respect to food, housing, work, and health care, and the provision of universal insurance;

m.   the attainment of self-sufficiency in industrial, agricultural, and military science, and technology, and all related matters;

n.   securing the comprehensive rights of all citizens, both women and men, and the establishment of judicial security for all, as well as the equality of all before the law;

o.   the expansion and strengthening of Islamic brotherhood and public cooperation among all the people;

p.   the formulation of the foreign policy of the country on the basis of Islamic criteria, brotherly commitment to all Muslims, and the unstinting support of all oppressed and deprived people throughout the world.

ARTICLE 4

All civil, penal, financial, economic, administrative, cultural, military, political, and other laws and regulations must be based on Islamic criteria. This principle applies absolutely and generally to all articles of the Constitution as well as to all laws and regulations, and the *fuqaha* on the Council of Guardians have the duty of supervising its implementation.

ARTICLE 5

During the Occultation of the Lord of the Age (may God hasten his renewed manifestation!), the governance and leadership of the nation devolve upon the just and pious *faqih* who is acquainted with the circumstances of his age; courageous, resourceful, and possessed of administrative ability; and recognized and accepted as leader by the majority of the people. In the event that no *faqih* should be so recognized by the majority, the leader, or the Leadership Council, composed of *fuqaha* possessing the aforementioned qualifications, will assume these responsibilities in accordance with Article 107.

ARTICLE 6

In the Islamic Republic of Iran, the affairs of the country must be administered on the basis of public opinion expressed by means of elections, including the election of the President of the Republic, the representatives of the National Consultative Assembly, and the members of councils, or by means of referenda in matters specified in other articles of this Constitution.

ARTICLE 7

In accordance with the command of the Qur'an contained in the verses *"Their affairs are by consultation among them"* (42:38) and *"Consult them on affairs"* (3:159), councils and consultative bodies—such as the National Consultative Assembly, the Provincial Councils, the Municipal Councils, and the City, Neighborhood, Division, and Village Councils—belong to the decision-making and administrative organs of the country.

The nature of these councils, together with the manner of their formation and the limits of their powers and functions, is determined by the Constitution and laws arising from it.

ARTICLE 8

In the Islamic Republic of Iran, summoning men to good by enjoining good and forbidding evil is a universal and mutual duty that must be fulfilled by the people with respect to each other, by the government with respect to the people, and by the people with respect to the government. The conditions, limits, and nature of this duty will be specified by law. This is in accordance with the Qur'anic verse *"The believers, men and women, are the protectors of each other; they enjoin the good and forbid the evil"* (9:71).

ARTICLE 9

In the Islamic Republic of Iran, the freedom, independence, unity, and territorial integrity of the country are inseparable from each other, and their preservation is the duty of the government and of all individual citizens. No individual, group, or authority has the right to infringe in the slightest way upon the political, cultural, economic, and military independence or the territorial integrity of Iran under the pretext of exercising freedom. Similarly, no authority has the right to withdraw legitimate freedoms, even by establishing laws and regulations for that purpose, under the pretext of preserving the independence and territorial integrity of the country.

ARTICLE 10

In accordance with the verse *"This your nation is a single nation, and I am your Lord, so worship Me,"* all Muslims form a single nation, and the government of the Islamic Republic of Iran has the duty of formulating its general policies with a view to the merging and union of all Muslim peoples, and it must constantly strive to bring about the political, economic, and cultural unity of the Islamic world.

ARTICLE 11

Since the family is the fundamental unit of Islamic society, all pertinent laws, regulations, and programs must tend to facilitate the foundation of a family and to protect the sanctity and stability of family relations on the basis of the law and the ethics of Islam.

ARTICLE 12

The official religion of Iran is Islam and the Twelver Ja'fari school of thought, and this principle shall remain eternally immutable. Other Islamic schools of thought, including the Hanafi, Shafi'i, Maliki, Hanbali, and Zaydi schools, are to be accorded full respect, and their followers are free to act in accordance with their own jurisprudence in performing their religious devotions. These schools enjoy official status for the purposes of religious education and matters of personal status (marriage, divorce, inheritance, and bequests), being accepted in the courts for cases relating to such matters. In areas of the country where Muslims following one of these schools of thought constitute the majority, local regulations, within the bounds of the jurisdiction of local councils, are to be in accordance with the respective school of thought, without infringing upon the rights of the followers of other schools.

ARTICLE 13

Zoroastrian, Jewish, and Christian Iranians are the only recognized religious minorities, with the right freely to perform their religious ceremonies within the limits of the law and to act according to their own customs in matters of personal status and religious education.

ARTICLE 14

In accordance with the verse *"God does not forbid you to deal kindly and justly with those who have not fought against you because of your religion and who have not expelled you from your homes"* (60:8), the government of the Islamic Republic of Iran and all Muslims are duty-bound to treat non-Muslims in an ethical fashion and in accordance with Islamic justice and equity and to respect their human rights. This principle applies to all who refrain from engaging in conspiracy or activity against Islam and the Islamic Republic of Iran.

Chapter II
The Language, Script, Calendar, and Flag of the Country

ARTICLE 15

The official language and script of Iran, the lingua franca of its people, is Persian. Official documents, correspondence, and texts as well as schoolbooks must be in this language and script. The use of regional and national (*qaumi*) languages in the press and mass media, however, as well as for teaching in schools the literatures written in them, is permitted in addition to Persian.

ARTICLE 16

Since the language of the Qur'an and of Islamic learning and culture is Arabic, and since Persian literature has been thoroughly permeated by this language, it must be taught in all classes from elementary school through middle school, and in all areas of study.

ARTICLE 17

The official calendar of the country takes as its point of departure the migration of the Prophet of Islam—God's peace and blessings upon him and his family! Both the solar and the lunar Islamic calendars are recognized, but government offices will base their operations on the solar calendar. The official weekly holiday is Friday.

ARTICLE 18

The official flag of Iran is green, white, and red and bears the special emblem of the Islamic Republic together with the words *"Allahu Akbar."*

Chapter III
The Rights of the People

ARTICLE 19

Whatever the ethnic group or tribe to which they belong, all people of Iran enjoy equal rights, and factors such as color, race, and language do not bestow any privilege.

ARTICLE 20

All citizens of the nation, both women and men, equally enjoy the protection of the law and enjoy all human, political, economic, social, and cultural rights, in conformity with Islamic criteria.

ARTICLE 21

The government must assure the rights of women in all respects, in conformity with Islamic criteria, and accomplish the following goals:

a.   create a favorable environment for the growth of woman's personality and the restoration of her rights, tangible and intangible;

b. the protection of mothers, particularly during pregnancy and childrearing, and the protection of children without guardians;

c. the creation of a competent court to protect and preserve the family;

d. the provision of special insurance for widows and aged and destitute women;

e. the granting of guardianship of children to their mothers whenever suitable in order to protect the interests of the children, in the absence of a legal guardian.

ARTICLE 22

The dignity, life, property, rights, dwelling, and occupation of the individual are inviolate, except in cases sanctioned by the law.

ARTICLE 23

The interrogation of persons concerning their opinions is forbidden, and no one may be molested or taken to task simply for holding a certain opinion.

ARTICLE 24

Publications and the press are free to present all matters except those that are detrimental to the fundamental principles of Islam or the rights of the public. The details of this exception will be specified by the law.

ARTICLE 25

The inspection of letters and the failure to deliver them, the recording and disclosure of telephone conversations,

the disclosure of telegraphic and telex communications
or the willful failure to transmit them, wiretapping, and
all forms of covert investigation are forbidden, except
as provided by law.

ARTICLE 26

The formation of political and professional parties,
associations, and societies, as well as religious societies,
whether they be Islamic or pertain to one of the recognized religious minorities, is freely permitted on condition that they do not violate the principles of independence, freedom, national unity, the criteria of Islam, or
the basis of the Islamic Republic. No one may be prevented from participating in the aforementioned groups,
or be compelled to participate in them.

ARTICLE 27

Public gatherings and marches may freely be held, on
condition that arms are not carried and that they are not
detrimental to the fundamental principles of Islam.

ARTICLE 28

Everyone has the right to choose any employment he
wishes, if it is not opposed to Islam, the public interest,
or the rights of others. The government has the duty,
while bearing in mind the needs of society for different
kinds of work, to provide every citizen with the opportunity to work, and to create equal conditions for obtaining it.

ARTICLE 29

The right to benefit from social security with respect to retirement, unemployment, old age, disability, and destitution benefits, as well as benefits relating to being stranded and emergencies, health services, medicine, and medical care, provided through insurance or other means, is a universal right.

The government must assure the foregoing rights and financial protection by drawing on the national income, in accordance with the law, and on income derived from the participation of the people.

ARTICLE 30

The government must provide all citizens with free education to the end of middle school, and must expand higher education to the level required by the country for self-sufficiency.

ARTICLE 31

To own a dwelling commensurate with one's needs is the right of every individual and family in Iran. The government must make land available for the implementation of this principle, according priority to those whose need is greatest, in particular the rural population and the workers.

ARTICLE 32

No one can be arrested except in accordance with judgment and the procedure established by law. In the case of arrest, charges and supporting evidence must be communicated immediately in writing to the prisoner and be elucidated to him, and a provisional dossier must be forwarded to the competent judicial authorities within a maximum of twenty-four hours so that the preliminaries to the trial can be completed as swiftly as possible. Punishments for the infringement of these principles will be determined by law.

ARTICLE 33

No one can be banished from his place of residence, prevented from residing in his preferred location, or compelled to reside in a given locality, except as provided in law.

ARTICLE 34

It is the indisputable right of every citizen to seek justice, and everyone may have access to the competent courts in order to present his case. All members of the nation have the right of access to such courts, and no one can be barred from courts to which they have a legal right of recourse.

ARTICLE 35

Both parties to a dispute have the right in all courts of law to select a lawyer, and if they are unable to do so, arrangements must be made to provide them with legal counsel.

ARTICLE 36

The passing and execution of sentence must be performed only by the appropriate court and in accordance with law.

ARTICLE 37

Innocence is to be presumed, and no one is to be regarded as guilty unless his guilt has been established by the competent court.

ARTICLE 38

Any form of torture for the purpose of extracting confessions or gaining information is forbidden. It is not permissible to compel individuals to give testimony, make confessions, or swear oaths, and any testimony, confession, or oath obtained in this fashion is worthless and invalid. Punishments for the infringement of these principles will be determined by law.

ARTICLE 39

All affronts to the dignity and honor of persons arrested, detained, imprisoned, or banished in accordance with the law, whatever form they may take, are forbidden and punishable.

ARTICLE 40

No one can make the exercise of his rights a pretext for harming others or encroaching on the public interest.

ARTICLE 41

Iranian nationality is the indisputable right of every Iranian, and the government cannot withdraw nationality from any Iranian unless he himself requests it or acquires the nationality of another country.

ARTICLE 42

Foreign nationals may acquire Iranian nationality within the framework of the relevant laws. Nationality may be withdrawn from such persons if another state accepts them as its nationals or if they request it.

Chapter IV
Economy and Financial Affairs

ARTICLE 43

In order that the economic independence of society may be secured, poverty and deprivation uprooted, and the needs of man in his process of growth and advancement satisfied, while at the same time preserving his liberty, the economy of the Islamic Republic of Iran is to be based on the following criteria:

a.   the provision of basic necessities to all citizens: accommodation, food, clothing, health care, medicine, education, and the necessary facilities for the establishment of a family;

b.   assuring conditions and possibilities of employment for everyone, with a view to attaining full employment; placing the means of labor at the disposal of everyone who is able to work but lacks the means, in the form of cooperatives; and granting interest-free loans or recourse to any other legitimate means that neither results in the concentration of wealth in the hands of a few individuals or its circulation among them nor turns the government into a major or dominant employer. These steps must be taken with due regard for the necessities determining public planning of the national economy at each stage of its growth;

c.   the drawing up of the economic plan for the country in such a manner that the form, content, and hours of work of every individual will leave him, in addition to his labor, sufficient opportunity and strength to engage in intellectual, political, and social self-development, active participation in the leadership of the country, and the improvement of his skills and sense of initiative;

d.   respect for the right to choose freely one's job; refraining from compelling anyone to engage in a particular job; and preventing the exploitation of another's labor;

e.   forbidding the infliction of harm upon others, monopoly, hoarding, usury, and other evil and forbidden practices;

f.   the prohibition of extravagance and wastefulness in all matters related to the economy, including consumption, investment, production, distribution, and services;

g.   the utilization of science and technology, and the training of skilled individuals in accordance with need for the sake of the development and progress of the country's economy;

h.   prevention of foreign economic domination over the country's economy;

i.   emphasis on the increase of agricultural, livestock, and industrial production in order to satisfy public needs and to make the country self-sufficient and independent.

ARTICLE 44

The economic system of the Islamic Republic of Iran is to consist of three sectors: state, cooperative, and private, and is to be based on orderly and correct planning.

The state sector is to include all large-scale and major industries, foreign trade, major mineral resources, banking, insurance, energy, dams and large-scale irrigation networks, radio and television, post, telegraphic and telephone services, aviation, shipping, roads, railroads and the like; all these will be publicly owned and administered by the state.

The cooperative sector is to include cooperative companies and institutions concerned with production and distribution, established in both the cities and the countryside, in accordance with Islamic criteria.

The private sector consists of those activities concerned with agriculture, animal husbandry, industry, trade, and services that supplement the economic activities of the state and cooperative sectors.

Ownership in each of these three sectors is protected by the laws of the Islamic Republic, to the extent permitted by the other articles of this chapter, and on condition that such ownership does not go beyond the bounds of Islamic law, that it contributes to the economic growth and progress of the country, and that it does not harm society.

The [precise] scope of each of the three sectors, as well as the regulations and conditions governing their operation, will be specified by law.

ARTICLE 45

Public wealth and property, such as uncultivated or abandoned land, minerals, seas, lakes, rivers and other public bodies of water, mountains, valleys, forests, marshland, natural forests, unenclosed pastureland, legacies without heirs, property of undetermined ownership, and public property recovered from usurpers, shall be at the disposal of the Islamic government for it to use in accordance with the public interest. Law will specify detailed arrangements for the utilization of each of the foregoing items.

ARTICLE 46

Everyone is the owner of the fruits of his legitimate business and labor, and no one may deprive another of the opportunity of work under the pretext of this ownership.

ARTICLE 47

Private ownership, legitimately achieved, is to be respected. The relevant criteria are determined by law.

ARTICLE 48

All forms of discrimination among the various provinces must be avoided in the exploitation of natural resources, in the utilization of public income, and in the distribution of economic activities among the various provinces and regions of the country, thereby ensuring that every region has access to the necessary capital and facilities in accordance with its needs and capacity for growth.

ARTICLE 49

The government has the responsibility of confiscating all wealth resulting from usury, usurpation, bribery, embezzlement, theft, gambling, misuse of endowments, misuse of government contracts and transactions, the sale of uncultivated lands and other categories of land inherently subject to public ownership, the operation of houses of ill-repute, and other illicit sources. When appropriate, such wealth must be restored to its legitimate owner, and if no such owner can be identified, it must be placed in the public treasury. The application of this principle must be accompanied by due investigation and verification in accordance with the law of Islam and carried out by the government.

ARTICLE 50

The preservation of the environment in which present and future generations are charged with the construction of a progressive society is regarded as a public duty in the Islamic Republic. Economic and other activities that tend consistently to pollute the environment or inflict irreparable damage on it are therefore forbidden.

ARTICLE 51

No form of taxation may be imposed except in accordance with the law. Provisions for tax exemption and reduction will be determined by law.

ARTICLE 52

The annual budget of the country will be drawn up by the government, in the manner specified by law, and submitted to the National Consultative Assembly for discussion and approval. Any change in the figures contained in the budget will be in accordance with the procedures established in law.

ARTICLE 53

All sums received by the government will be concentrated in accounts at the central treasury, and all disbursements shall be within the allocations approved in accordance with law.

ARTICLE 54

The National Accounting Agency is to be directly under the supervision of the National Consultative Assembly. Its organization and mode of operation, in Tehran and in provincial centers, are to be determined by law.

ARTICLE 55

The Accounting Agency will investigate and/or audit, in the manner prescribed by law, all the accounts of ministries, state institutions, and companies that benefit in any way from the general budget of the country. It will ensure that no expenditure exceeds the allocations approved and that all sums are spent for the proper purpose. It will collect all relevant accounts, bills, records, and documents, in accordance with law, and submit to the National Consultative Assembly a report for the settlement of each year's budget together with its own comments. This report must be made available to the public.

Chapter V
The Right of National Sovereignty and the Powers Deriving Therefrom

ARTICLE 56

Absolute sovereignty over the world and man belongs to God, and it is He Who has placed man in charge of his social destiny. No one can deprive man of this God-given right, nor subordinate it to the interests of a given individual or group. The people exercise this God-given right by the paths specified in the articles below.

ARTICLE 57

The powers of government in the Islamic Republic consist of the legislative, the judiciary, and the executive powers, functioning under the supervision of those invested with governance and leadership and in accordance with articles of this Constitution. These powers are independent of each other, and communication among them will be ensured by the President of the Republic.

ARTICLE 58

The exercise of the legislative power is by means of the National Consultative Assembly, consisting of the elected representatives of the people. Legislation approved by this body, after completion of the stages specified in the articles below, is communicated to the executive and the judiciary for implementation.

ARTICLE 59

In economic, political, social, and cultural matters of great importance, it is possible for the legislative power to be exercised by means of a referendum and direct consultation with the people to determine their views. Any request for such direct consultation must be approved by two-thirds of the members of the National Consultative Assembly.

ARTICLE 60

The exercise of the executive power is by means of the President of the Republic, the Prime Minister, and the ministers, except for matters directly assigned to the leadership by this Constitution.

ARTICLE 61

The exercise of the judiciary power is by means of courts of justice, which are to be formed in accordance with the criteria of Islam and are to examine and settle cases, protect the rights of the public, dispense and enact justice, and establish the divine limits.

Chapter VI
The Legislative Power

Section One
The National Consultative Assembly

ARTICLE 62

The National Consultative Assembly consists of the representatives of the people elected directly and by secret ballot.

The qualifications of electors and candidates, as well as the method of election, will be specified by law.

ARTICLE 63

The term of membership in the National Consultative Assembly is four years. Elections for each term must take place before the end of the preceding term, so that the country is never without an Assembly.

ARTICLE 64

There are to be two hundred seventy members of the National Consultative Assembly. After every ten years, if the population of the country has increased, representatives will be added to each electoral district at the rate of one per every 150,000 additional persons. The Zoroastrians and Jews will each elect one representative; Assyrian and Chaldean Christians will jointly elect one representative; and Armenian Christians in the north and those in the south of the country will each elect one representative. If the population of these minorities increases, they will be given additional representatives at the rate of one per 150,000. Regulations concerning elections will be established by law.

ARTICLE 65

After the holding of elections, sessions of the National Consultative Assembly are considered legal when two-thirds of the total members are present. Drafts and bills presented to the Assembly will be approved in accordance with the internal protocol approved by it, except in cases where the Constitution has specified a certain quorum. The agreement of two-thirds of all members present is necessary for the approval of the internal protocol of the Assembly.

ARTICLE 66

The manner of election of the president and governing body of the Assembly, the number of commissions and their term of office, and matters relating to the discussions and disciplinary regulations of the Assembly will be determined by the internal protocols of the Assembly.

ARTICLE 67

Members of the Assembly must swear the following oath at the first session of the Assembly and affix their signatures to its text:

In the Name of God, the Compassionate, the Merciful

In the presence of the Glorious Qur'an, I swear by God, the Powerful and Almighty, and undertake, relying upon my honor as a human being, to protect the sanctity of Islam and guard the accomplishments of the Islamic Revolution of the Iranian people and the foundations of the Islamic Republic; to protect, as just trustee, the trust bestowed upon me by the people; to observe piety in fulfilling my duties as a member of the assembly; to be constantly devoted to the independence and advancement of the country, the protection of the rights of the nation, and the service of the people; to defend the Constitution; and to bear in mind, both in speech and writing and in the expression of opinion, the independence of the country, the freedom of the people, and the securing of their interests.

Members belonging to the religious minorities will mention their own sacred books when swearing this oath.

Members not participating in the first session will perform the ceremony of swearing the oath at the first session they attend.

ARTICLE 68

In time of war and the military occupation of the country, elections due to be held in occupied areas or nationwide may be delayed for a specified period if proposed by the President of the Republic, and approved by three-fourths of the total members of the National Consultative Assembly, with the endorsement of the Council of Guardians. If a new Assembly cannot be formed, the previous one will continue to function.

ARTICLE 69

The deliberations of the National Consultative Assembly must be held in public, and a full report of them made available to the public by the radio and the official gazette. A closed session may be held in emergencies, if it is required for national security, upon the demand of the Prime Minister, one of the ministers, or ten members of the Assembly. Legislation passed at a closed session is valid only when approved by three-fourths of the members in the presence of the Council of Guardians. After emergency conditions have ceased to apply, the minutes of such closed sessions, together with any legislation approved in them, must be made available to the public.

ARTICLE 70

The President, the Prime Minister, and the ministers have the right to participate in the open sessions of the Assembly either collectively or individually. If the members of the Assembly deem it necessary, the President of the Republic, the Prime Minister, and the ministers are obliged to attend. Conversely, whenever they request it, their statements are to be heard.

Any invitation to the President of the Republic to attend the Assembly must be approved by a majority of the members.

Section Two
Powers and Authority of the National Consultative Assembly

ARTICLE 71

The National Consultative Assembly can establish laws on all matters, within the limits of its competence as laid down in the Constitution.

ARTICLE 72

The National Consultative Assembly cannot enact laws contrary to the principles and ordinances of the official religion of the country or to the Constitution. It is the duty of the Council of Guardians to determine whether a violation has occurred, in accordance with Article 96.

ARTICLE 73

The interpretation of ordinary laws falls within the competence of the National Consultative Assembly. The intent of this Article does not prevent the interpretations that judges may make in the course of cassation.

ARTICLE 74

Bills are presented to the National Consultative Assembly after receiving the approval of the Council of Ministers. Draft bills may be introduced in the National Consultative Assembly if sponsored by at least fifteen members.

ARTICLE 75

Drafts, proposals, and amendments to bills already proposed by members that entail the reduction of the public income or the increase of public expenditure may be introduced in the Assembly only if means for compensating for the decrease in income or for securing the new expenditure are also specified.

ARTICLE 76

The National Consultative Assembly has the right to investigate and examine all the affairs of the country.

ARTICLE 77

Treaties, international undertakings, and other agreements of a similar nature must be approved by the National Consultative Assembly.

ARTICLE 78

All changes in the boundaries of the country are forbidden, with the exception of minor rectifications in keeping with the interests of the country, on condition that they are not unilateral, do not encroach on the independence and territorial integrity of the country, and receive the approval of four-fifths of the total members of the National Consultative Assembly.

ARTICLE 79

The establishment of martial law is forbidden. In case of war or emergency conditions akin to war, the government has the right to impose temporarily certain essential restrictions, with the agreement of the National Consultative Assembly. In no case can such restrictions last for more than thirty days; if the need for them persists beyond thirty days, the government must obtain new authorization for them from the Assembly.

ARTICLE 80

The taking and giving of loans or grants-in-aid, domestic and foreign, must be approved by the National Consultative Assembly.

ARTICLE 81

The granting of concessions to foreigners for the formation of companies or institutions for commercial, industrial, and agricultural purposes, or for the extraction of minerals, is absolutely forbidden.

ARTICLE 82

The employment of foreign experts is forbidden, except in cases of necessity and with the approval of the National Consultative Assembly.

ARTICLE 83

Government buildings and properties forming part of the national patrimony cannot be transferred except with the approval of the National Consultative Assembly; unique and irreplaceable treasures are not covered by this exception.

ARTICLE 84

Every member is responsible to the entire nation, and has the right to express his opinion on all matters of domestic and foreign policy.

ARTICLE 85

Membership in the National Consultative Assembly applies to the individual and cannot be delegated. The Assembly cannot assign the power of legislation to a single individual or to a group. In cases of overriding need, however, it can delegate the establishment of certain categories of law to its internal commissions, in accordance with Article 72. In such a case, the laws will be executed on an experimental basis for a period specified by the Assembly, and their final approval will depend on the Assembly [as a whole].

ARTICLE 86

Members of the Assembly are completely free to express their views in the course of performing their duties as members, and they cannot be prosecuted or arrested for opinions expressed in the Assembly or views uttered [elsewhere] in the course of performing their duty.

ARTICLE 87

The Council of Ministers, after being formed and presented to the Assembly and before all other business, must obtain a vote of confidence from the Assembly. During its incumbency, it can also request a vote of confidence from the Assembly on important questions or matters being disputed.

ARTICLE 88

Whenever a member of the Assembly poses a question to a minister on a subject relating to his duties, the minister is obliged to attend the Assembly and answer the question. His answer must not be delayed more than ten days, except with an excuse deemed valid by the National Consultative Assembly.

ARTICLE 89

Members of the Assembly can interpellate the Council of Ministers or an individual minister in instances they deem necessary. Interpellations can be tabled if they bear the signatures of ten members. The Council of Ministers or interpellated minister must be present in the Assembly within ten days after the tabling of the interpellation in order to answer it and seek a vote of confidence. If the Council of Ministers or the minister concerned fails to attend the Assembly, the members who tabled the interpellation will explain their reasons, and the Assembly will declare a vote of no confidence if it deems it necessary.

If the Assembly does not give a vote of confidence, the Council of Ministers or minister subject to interpellation is dismissed. In both cases, the Prime Minister and the ministers subject to interpellation cannot participate in the next Council of Ministers to be formed.

ARTICLE 90

Whoever has a complaint concerning the work of the Assembly, the executive power, or the judicial power can present his complaint in writing to the Assembly. The Assembly must investigate his complaint and give an adequate response. In cases where the complaint relates to the executive or the judiciary, the Assembly must demand investigation and the furnishing of an adequate response from them, and announce the results within a reasonable time. In cases where the subject of the complaint is of public interest, the result must be made public.

ARTICLE 91

In order to protect the ordinances of Islam and the Constitution by assuring that legislation passed by the National Consultative Assembly does not conflict with them, a council to be known as the Council of Guardians is to be established with the following composition:

a.   six just *fuqaha,* conscious of current needs and the issues of the day, to be selected by the leader or the Leadership Council; and
b.   six jurists, specializing in different areas of law, to be elected by the National Consultative Assembly from among the Muslim jurists presented to it by the Supreme Judicial Council.

ARTICLE 92

Members of the Council of Guardians are selected to serve for a period of six years, but during the first term, after three years have passed, two members of each group will be changed by lottery and new members will be selected in their place.

ARTICLE 93

The National Consultative Assembly does not have legal validity if there is no Council of Guardians in existence other than to approve the credentials of its members and select the six jurists who are to sit on the Council of Guardians.

ARTICLE 94

All legislation passed by the National Consultative Assembly must be sent to the Council of Guardians. The Council of Guardians must review it within a maximum of ten days from its receipt with a view to ensuring its compatibility with the criteria of Islam and the Constitution. If it finds the legislation not so compatible, it will return it to the Assembly for review. If the Council fails to do the foregoing, legislation passed by the Assembly acquires the force of law.

ARTICLE 95

In cases where the Council of Guardians deems ten days inadequate for completing the process of review and delivering a definitive opinion, it can request an extension of not more than ten days from the National Consultative Assembly, stating its reason for the request.

ARTICLE 96

The determination of whether legislation passed by the National Consultative Assembly is compatible with the ordinances of Islam depends on a majority vote by the *fuqaha* on the Council of Guardians; and the determination that it is compatible with the Constitution requires a majority vote by all members of the Council of Guardians.

ARTICLE 97

In order to accelerate their work, the members of the Council of Guardians may attend the Assembly and listen to its debates when a bill or draft is under discussion. When an urgent draft or bill has been inscribed on the agenda of the Assembly, the members of the Council of Guardians must attend the Assembly and make their views known.

ARTICLE 98

The interpretation of the Constitution is the responsibility of the Council of Guardians, and depends on the approval of three-fourths of its members.

ARTICLE 99

The Council of Guardians has the responsibility of supervising the election of the President of the Republic, the elections for the National Consultative Assembly, and the direct consultation of popular opinion and referenda.

Chapter VII
Councils

ARTICLE 100

In order to carry forward swiftly social, economic, development, public health, cultural, and educational programs, as well as other projects promoting the well-being of society, in collaboration with the people and with regard for local administrative needs in each village, division, city, municipality, and province, the administration of each village, division, city, municipality, and province will be supervised by a council to be known as the Village, Division, City, Municipality, or Provincial Council. The members of each of these councils will be elected by the people of the locality in question.

Qualifications for the electors and candidates for these councils, as well as their functions and powers, the method of election to them, the way in which they exercise their supervision, and the chain of authority that is to exist among them, will be determined by law, in such a way as to preserve national unity, territorial integrity, the system of the Islamic Republic, and the primacy of the central government.

ARTICLE 101

In order to prevent discrimination and attract the co-operation [of the people] in the preparation of programs for the development and prosperity of the provinces and in the harmonious implementation of such programs, a Supreme Council of the Provinces will be formed, composed of representatives of the Provincial Councils. Law will specify the manner in which this council is to be formed and the functions that it is to fulfill.

ARTICLE 102

The Supreme Council of the Provinces has the right, within the limits of its power, to prepare draft plans and to submit them to the National Consultative Assembly, either directly or by way of the government. These drafts must be examined by the Assembly.

ARTICLE 103

Provincial governors, city governors, divisional governors, and other officials appointed by the government must respect all decisions taken by the councils within the limits of their powers.

ARTICLE 104

In order to ensure Islamic equity and collaboration in the preparation of programs and to bring about the harmonious progress of all units of production, both industrial and agricultural, councils consisting of the representatives of the workers, peasants, other employees, and managers, will be formed. In educational, administrative, service, and other units, similar councils will be formed, composed of representatives of the members of those units.

The manner in which these councils are to be formed, together with their functions and powers, is to be specified by law.

ARTICLE 105

Decisions taken by the councils must not contradict the criteria of Islam and the laws of the country.

ARTICLE 106

The councils may not be dissolved unless they deviate from their legal duties. The body responsible for determining whether such deviation has occurred, as well as the manner for dissolving the councils and re-forming them, will be specified by law.

Chapter VIII
The Leader or Leadership Council

ARTICLE 107

Whenever one of the *fuqaha* possessing the qualifications specified in Article 5 of the Constitution is recognized and accepted as *marja'* and leader by a decisive majority of the people—as has been the case with the exalted *marja'-i taqlid* and leader of the revolution, Ayatullah al-Uzma Imam Khomeini—he is to exercise governance and all the responsibilities arising therefrom. If such should not be the case, experts elected by the people will review and consult among themselves concerning all persons qualified to act as *marja'* and leader. If they discern outstanding capacity for leadership in a certain *marja'*, they will present him to the people as their leader; if not, they will appoint either three or five *marja'*'s possessing the necessary qualifications for leadership and present them as members of the Leadership Council.

ARTICLE 108

The law setting out the number and qualifications of the experts [mentioned in the preceding article], the manner of their election, and the internal protocol regulating the sessions of their first term must be drawn up by the *fuqaha* on the first Council of Guardians, and be approved by a majority among them and then by the Leader of the Revolution. Any subsequent change or review of the law [in question] may be undertaken by the Assembly of Experts.

ARTICLE 109

The following are the qualifications and attributes of the leader or members of the Leadership Council:

a. suitability with respect to learning and piety, as required for the functions of *mufti* and *marja'*;
b. political and social perspicacity, courage, strength, and the necessary administrative abilities for leadership.

ARTICLE 110

The leadership is to be assigned the following duties and powers:

a. appointment of the *fuqaha* on the Council of Guardians;
b. appointment of the supreme judicial authority of the country;
c. supreme command of the armed forces, exercised in the following manner:
>   (i)   appointment and dismissal of the chief of the general staff;
>   (ii) appointment and dismissal of the commander-in-chief of the Corps of Guards of the Islamic Revolution;

(iii) the formation of a Supreme National Defense Council, composed of the following seven members:
- the President
- the Prime Minister
- the minister of defense
- the chief of the general staff
- the commander-in-chief of the Corps of Guards of the Islamic Revolution
- two advisers appointed by the leader

(iv) appointment of the supreme commanders of the three branches of the armed forces, based upon the recommendation of the Supreme National Defense Council;

(v) the declaration of war and peace, and the mobilization of the armed forces, based on the recommendation of the Supreme National Defense Council;

d. signing the decree [formalizing the election] of the President of the Republic after his election by the people. The suitability of candidates for the presidency of the Republic, with respect to the qualifications specified in the Constitution, must be confirmed before elections take place by the Council of Guardians, and, in the case of the first term, by the leadership.

e. dismissal of the President of the Republic, with due regard for the interests of the country, after the issue of a judgment by the Supreme Court convicting him of failure to fulfill his legal duties, or a vote of the National Consultative Assembly testifying to his political incompetence;

f. pardoning or reducing the sentences of convicts, within the bounds of Islamic criteria, after receiving a recommendation [to that effect] from the Supreme Court.

ARTICLE 111

Whenever the leader or one member of the Leadership Council becomes incapable of fulfilling the legal duties of leadership, or loses one of the qualifications mentioned in Article 109, he will be dismissed. Determination [of the necessity of such dismissal] will be made by the experts mentioned in Article 108.

Regulations for the convening of the experts in order to implement this provision will be established at the first session of the Assembly of Experts.

ARTICLE 112

The leader or the members of the Leadership Council are equal before the law with all other citizens.

Chapter IX
The Executive Power

Section One
The Presidency

ARTICLE 113

After the leadership, the President of the Republic is the highest official position in the country. His is the responsibility for implementing the Constitution, ordering relations among the three powers, and heading the executive power except in matters pertaining directly to the leadership.

ARTICLE 114

The President of the Republic is elected for a four-year term by the direct consultation of the popular vote. He may be re-elected only once to serve a successive term.

ARTICLE 115

The President of the Republic must be elected from among religious and political personalities possessing the following qualifications:

Iranian origin; Iranian nationality; administrative and managerial capacities; a good past record; trustworthiness; piety; convinced belief in the fundamental principles of the Islamic Republic of Iran and the official school of thought of the country.

ARTICLE 116

Candidates for the post of President of the Republic must announce their candidacy officially. Law establishes the manner in which the President of the Republic is to be elected.

ARTICLE 117

The President of the Republic is elected by an absolute majority of votes of all participants [in the election]. But if none of the candidates is able to win such a majority in the first round of voting, voting will take place a second time on Friday of the following week. In the second round, only the two candidates who received the most votes in the first round will participate. If, however, some of the candidates who gained the most votes in the first round withdraw from the elections, the final choice will be between the two candidates who won more votes than all the remaining candidates.

ARTICLE 118

Responsibility for the supervision of the election of the President of the Republic lies with the Council of Guardians, as stipulated in Article 99. Before the establishment of the first Council of Guardians, however, it lies with a supervisory body to be established by law.

ARTICLE 119

The election of a new President of the Republic must take place no later than one month before the end of the term of the preceding President. In the interval between the election of the new President and the end of the term of the preceding President, the outgoing President performs the duties of President of the Republic.

ARTICLE 120

If any of the candidates whose suitability is established in terms of the qualifications listed above should die ten days before balloting day, the elections will be postponed for two weeks. If one of the candidates holding the most votes dies in the interval between the first and second rounds of voting, the period for holding [the second round of] the election will be extended for two weeks.

ARTICLE 121

The President of the Republic must swear and affix his signature to the following oath at a session of the National Consultative Assembly in the presence of the head of the Supreme Court and the members of the Council of Guardians of the Constitution:

In the Name of God, the Compassionate, the Merciful
As President of the Republic, I swear, in the presence of the Noble Qur'an and the people of Iran, by God, Powerful and Almighty, that I will guard the official school of thought of the country, the order of the Islamic Republic

and the Constitution of the country; that I will devote all my capacities and abilities to the fulfillment of the responsibilities that I have assumed; that I will devote myself to the service of the people, the advancement of the country, the propagation of religion and morality, and the support of truth and justice; that I will protect the freedom and dignity of all citizens and the rights that the Constitution has accorded the people; that in guarding the frontiers and the political, economic, and cultural independence of the country I will not shirk any necessary measure; that, seeking help from God and following the Prophet of Islam and the Immaculate Imams (peace be upon them), I will guard the power vested in me by the people as a sacred trust, as a pious and selfless trustee, and surrender it to whomever the people may elect after me.

ARTICLE 122

The President of the Republic is responsible to the people within the limits of his functions and powers. The manner in which possible violation of this responsibility is to be investigated will be determined by law.

ARTICLE 123

The President of the Republic has the responsibility of signing legislation approved by the Assembly or the result of a referendum after the legal procedures have been completed and it has been communicated to him. After signature, he must forward it to the responsible authorities for implementation.

ARTICLE 124

The President of the Republic will nominate a candidate for the post of Prime Minister, and after obtaining a vote of endorsement from the National Consultative Assembly, he will issue a decree appointing his Prime Minister.

ARTICLE 125

The President or his legal representative signs pacts, conventions, treaties, and other agreements concluded by the Iranian government with other governments, as well as agreements pertaining to international organizations, after obtaining the approval of the National Consultative Assembly.

ARTICLE 126

Statutes and governmental protocols will be communicated to the President of the Republic after being approved by the Council of Ministers. If he deems them contrary to law, he returns them to the Council of Ministers for review, stating his reasons for so doing.

ARTICLE 127

Whenever the President of the Republic considers it necessary, he may attend and preside over sessions of the Council of Ministers.

ARTICLE 128

The President of the Republic signs the credentials of ambassadors being sent to foreign countries and receives the credentials presented by the ambassadors of foreign countries.

ARTICLE 129

The award of state decorations is a prerogative of the President of the Republic.

ARTICLE 130

In case of the absence or illness of the President of the Republic, his duties will be performed by a council called the Temporary Presidential Council, consisting of the Prime Minister, the president of the National Consultative Assembly, and the president of the Supreme Court, on condition that the circumstances excusing the President last not longer than two months. Similarly, in case of the dismissal of the President, or if the term of one President has come to an end and various obstacles have prevented the election of a new President, the duties of the President of the Republic will also be exercised by this council.

ARTICLE 131

In the case of death, resignation, illness lasting longer than two months, dismissal of the President of the Republic, or similar circumstances, the Temporary Presidential Council must arrange for a new President of the Republic to be elected within a maximum of fifty days. During this period, it will carry out all the functions and powers of the President except the initiation of referenda.

ARTICLE 132

During the period when the functions of President of the Republic are assigned to the Temporary Presidential

Council, it is not possible to interpellate the government, to pass a vote of no confidence in it, or to undertake any steps for a review of the Constitution.

Section Two
The Prime Minister and Ministers

ARTICLE 133

Ministers will be appointed upon the proposal of the Prime Minister together with the approval of the President of the Republic, and will be presented to the Assembly for a vote of confidence.

The number of ministers and the limits of the power of each will be determined by law.

ARTICLE 134

The Prime Minister is the head of the Council of Ministers. He supervises the work of the ministers and takes all necessary measures to coordinate the decisions of the government. With the cooperation of the ministers, he determines the program and policies of the government and executes the law. The Prime Minister is responsible to the Assembly for the actions of his ministers.

ARTICLE 135

The Prime Minister retains his position as long as he enjoys the confidence of the Assembly. The resignation of the government is to be presented to the President of the Republic, and the Prime Minister is to continue his functions until a new government is appointed.

ARTICLE 136

Whenever the Prime Minister wishes to dismiss a minister and appoint another in his place, both the dismissal and the appointment must be approved by the President of the Republic, and a vote of confidence must be obtained from the Assembly for the new minister. If half the members of the Council of Ministers change after the government has received its vote of confidence from the Assembly, the government must seek a new vote of confidence from the Assembly.

ARTICLE 137

Each of the ministers is responsible for his duties to the Assembly, but in matters that have been approved by the Council of Ministers as a whole, he is also responsible for the actions of the others.

ARTICLE 138

In addition to instances in which the Council of Ministers or a single minister is given the responsibility for drawing up regulations for the implementation of laws, the Council of Ministers has the right to establish decrees, regulations, and protocols in order to fulfill its administrative duties, secure the implementation of laws, and organize administrative bodies. Each minister also has the right to establish regulations and issue circulars within the limits of his functions and with the approval of the

Council of Ministers. The content of all such regulations must not oppose the letter or the spirit of the law.

ARTICLE 139

The settling of litigation relating to public and state property and the referral thereof to arbitration is in every case dependent on the approval of the Council of Ministers, and the Assembly must be informed of these matters. In cases where one party to the dispute is a foreigner, as well as in important cases that are purely domestic, the approval of the Assembly must also be obtained. Law will specify the important cases intended here.

ARTICLE 140

Accusations of common crime against the President of the Republic, the Prime Minister, and the ministers will be investigated in common courts of justice after the approval of the National Consultative Assembly has been obtained.

ARTICLE 141

The President of the Republic, the Prime Minister, ministers, and government employees cannot hold more than one government position, and it is forbidden for them to hold any additional post in institutions of which all or a part of the capital belongs to the government or to public institutions, to be a member of the National Consultative Assembly, to practice the profession of attorney or legal adviser, or to be the president, managing director, or a member of the board of directors of any private company, with the exception of cooperative companies affiliated with government offices and institutions.

Educational positions in universities and research establishments are excepted from this rule.

In time of necessity, the Prime Minister may temporarily assume responsibility for certain ministries.

ARTICLE 142

The financial holdings of the leader or members of the Leadership Council, the Prime Minister, the President of the Republic, and ministers, as well as their spouses and offspring, are to be examined before and after their term of office by the Supreme Court, in order to ensure they have not increased in a fashion contrary to law.

Section Three

The Army and the Corps of Guards of the Revolution

ARTICLE 143

The Army of the Islamic Republic of Iran has the duty of guarding the independence and territorial integrity of the country, as well as the order of the Islamic Republic.

ARTICLE 144

The Army of the Islamic Republic of Iran must be an Islamic army, i.e., Islamic in its ideological inspiration and popular [in its orientation], and accept into its service individuals who believe in the aims of the Islamic Revolution and are ready to devote themselves to the achievement of those aims.

ARTICLE 145

No foreigner will be accepted into the Army or security forces of the country.

ARTICLE 146

The establishment of any kind of foreign military base in Iran, even for peaceful purposes, is forbidden.

ARTICLE 147

In time of peace, the government must utilize the personnel and technical equipment of the Army in relief operations, educational and productive enterprises, and the Reconstruction Jihad, while fully observing Islamic criteria and ensuring that such utilization does not harm the combat-readiness of the Army.

ARTICLE 148

All forms of personal use of military vehicles and equipment, as well as personal use of Army personnel as servants and chauffeurs or in similar capacities, are forbidden.

ARTICLE 149

Promotion and the withdrawal of military rank take place in accordance with law.

ARTICLE 150

The Corps of Guards of the Islamic Revolution, established in the early days of the triumph of the Revolution, is to be maintained in order that it may continue in its role of guarding the Revolution and its achievements. The duties of this Corps, together with its areas of responsibility, in relation to the duties and areas of responsibility of the other armed forces, are to be determined by law, with emphasis on brotherly cooperation and harmony among them.

ARTICLE 151

In accordance with the noble Qur'anic verse *"Prepare against them whatever force you are able to muster, and horses ready for battle, striking fear into God's enemy and your enemy, and others beyond them unknown to you but known to God"* (8:60), the government has the responsibility of providing a program of military training, together with all requisite facilities, for all of its citizens, in accordance with Islamic criteria, in such a way that all citizens will always be able to engage in the armed defense of the Islamic Republic of Iran. The possession of arms, however, requires the granting of permission by the competent authorities.

Chapter X
Foreign Policy

ARTICLE 152

The foreign policy of the Islamic Republic of Iran is based upon the rejection of all forms of domination, the preservation of the complete independence and territorial integrity of the country, the defense of the rights of all Muslims, non-alignment with respect to the hegemonist superpowers, and the maintenance of mutually peaceful relations with all non-belligerent states.

ARTICLE 153

Any form of agreement resulting in foreign domination over the natural resources, economy, army, or culture of the country, as well as other aspects of the national life, is forbidden.

ARTICLE 154

The Islamic Republic of Iran has as its ideal human happiness throughout human society, and considers the attainment of independence, freedom, and just government to be the right of all peoples in the world. While scrupulously refraining from all forms of aggressive intervention in the internal affairs of other nations, it therefore protects the just struggles of the oppressed and deprived in every corner of the globe.

ARTICLE 155

The government of the Islamic Republic of Iran may grant political asylum to those who seek it unless they are regarded as traitors and criminals according to the laws of Iran.

Chapter XI
The Judiciary

ARTICLE 156

The judiciary is an independent power, the protector of the rights of the individual and society, responsible for the implementation of justice, and entrusted with the following duties:

a. investigating and passing judgment on grievances, violations of rights, and complaints; the resolving of litigation; the settling of enmities; and the taking of all necessary decisions and measures in probate matters as the law may determine;

b. restoring public rights and promoting justice and legitimate freedoms;

c. supervising the correct enforcement of laws;

d. uncovering crimes; prosecuting, punishing, and chastising criminals; and enacting the penalties and provisions of the Islamic penal code;

e. taking suitable measures to prevent the occurrence of crime and to reform criminals.

ARTICLE 157

In order to fulfill the responsibilities of the judiciary, a council to be known as the Supreme Judicial Council will be established, which will be the highest judicial body and entrusted with the following responsibilities:

a. establishing the necessary procedures in the Ministry of Justice to fulfill the responsibilities specified in Article 156;

b. preparing bills on judicial matters appropriate to [the form of government of] the Islamic Republic;

c. employing just and worthy judges, dismissing and appointing them, changing their place of service, assigning them particular functions, promoting them, and carrying out similar administrative duties, in accordance with the law.

ARTICLE 158

The Supreme Judicial Council is to consist of five members:

a. the head of the Supreme Court;

b. the Prosecutor-General;

c. three judges of proven justice and possessing the quality of *mujtahid*, to be chosen by all the judges of the country.

The members of this council shall be chosen in the manner to be prescribed by law, for a period of five years, and there is no objection to their being reelected. The qualifications for candidates and electors will be specified by law.

ARTICLE 159

The Ministry of Justice is the official body to which all grievances and complaints are to be referred. The formation of courts and the definition of their competences is to be determined by law.

ARTICLE 160

The Minister of Justice has the responsibility for all matters concerning the relationship between the judiciary, on the one hand, and the executive and legislative, on the other hand. He will be chosen from among the individuals proposed to the Prime Minister by the Supreme Judicial Council.

ARTICLE 161

The Supreme Court is to be formed for the purpose of supervising the correct implementation of the laws, ensuring uniformity of judicial procedure, and fulfilling any other responsibilities assigned to it by law, on the basis of regulations to be established by the Supreme Judicial Council.

ARTICLE 162

The head of the Supreme Court and the Prosecutor-General must both be just *mujtahids* well versed in judicial matters. They will be nominated by the leadership for a period of five years, in consultation with the Supreme Judicial Council.

ARTICLE 163

The attributes and qualifications of judge will be determined by law, in accordance with the criteria of *fiqh*.

ARTICLE 164

A judge cannot be removed from the post he occupies except by trial and the establishment of guilt, or in consequence of a violation entailing his separation, whether temporarily or permanently. A judge's place of service or post cannot be changed without his consent, unless the interest of society determines otherwise, in accordance with a unanimous vote of the members of the Supreme Judicial Council. The periodic transfer and rotation of judges will be in accordance with general regulations to be established by law.

ARTICLE 165

Trials are to be held openly and members of the public may freely attend, unless the court determines that an open trial would be contrary to public morality or order, or, in the case of private disputes, both parties request that the hearings should not be open.

ARTICLE 166

The verdicts of courts must be accompanied by proofs and include mention of the articles, law, and principles in accordance with which they are delivered.

ARTICLE 167

The judge must attempt to find a basis for judgment for every case in the codified laws of the land. If he is unable to do so, he will issue a verdict based on reference to reputable Islamic sources or *fatvas*. He cannot refrain from examining cases and delivering a verdict on the pretext of silence, deficiency, brevity, or contradiction in the law.

ARTICLE 168

Political and press offenses will be tried openly and in the presence of a jury, in courts attached to the Ministry of Justice. The manner of selection, qualifications, and powers of the jury, as well as the definition of political offenses, will be established by law in accordance with Islamic criteria.

ARTICLE 169

No act or omission may be regarded as a crime on the basis of a law established subsequent to it.

ARTICLE 170

Judges of courts are obliged to refrain from executing statutes and protocols of the government that are in conflict with the laws or the provisions of Islam, or lie outside the competence of the executive power. Anyone has the right to demand the voiding of any such regulation from the Court of Administrative Justice.

ARTICLE 171

If an individual suffers moral or material harm as the result of a failure or error of the judge with respect to the subject matter of a case, the verdict delivered, or the implementation of the verdict, the judge must stand surety for the reparation of that harm in accordance with Islamic criteria, if it be a case of failure. Otherwise, losses will be compensated for by the state. In all cases, the repute and good standing of the individual will be restored.

ARTICLE 172

Military courts will be established by law to investigate crimes committed in connection with their military or security duties by members of the Army, the gendarmerie, the police, and the Corps of Guards of the Islamic Revolution. They will be tried in common courts, however, for common crimes or crimes committed while implementing the directives of the Ministry of Justice. The office of military prosecutor and the military courts form part of the judiciary and are subject to the same principles that regulate the [entire] judiciary.

ARTICLE 173

In order to investigate the complaints, grievances, and objections of the people with respect to government officials, organs, and statutes, a court will be established to be known as the Court of Administrative Justice. The jurisdiction, powers, and mode of operation of this court will be established by law.

ARTICLE 174

Based on the right of the judiciary to supervise the proper functioning of affairs and the correct implementation of laws by the administrative organs of the government, an organization will be established under the supervision of the Supreme Judicial Council to be known as the National General Inspectorate. The powers and duties of this organization will be determined by law.

Chapter XII
Mass Media

ARTICLE 175

The free diffusion of information and views, in accordance with Islamic criteria, must be assured in the mass media (radio and television). The media are to be administered under the joint supervision of the three powers—the judiciary (Supreme Judicial Council), the legislative, and the executive—in a manner to be determined by law.

The Constitution of the Islamic Republic of Iran, drawn up in twelve chapters containing one hundred seventy-five articles and approved by a two-thirds majority of all members of the Assembly convened to subject the Constitution to definitive review, was definitively approved on the twenty-fourth day of Aban in the year 1358 of the solar Islamic calendar, corresponding to the twenty-fourth day of Dhilhijja in the year 1399 of the lunar Islamic calendar [November 15, 1979].

Glossary

"Allahu akbar": "God is the greatest."

faqih: a scholar of the Islamic religious sciences, especially jurisprudence.

fatva: authoritative expression of opinion on a question of religious law, delivered by a religious scholar possessing the necessary qualifications.

fiqh: jurisprudence; the study and elaboration of Islamic law.

fuqaha: plural of *faqih.*

ijtihad: the deduction of particular applications of Islamic law from its sources and general principles by a religious scholar who possesses the appropriate qualifications.

maraji'-i taqlid: plural of *marja'-i taqlid.*

marja'-i taqlid: a *mujtahid* whose authoritative guidance is followed in matters of Islamic practice and law.

ma'sumin: those divinely endowed with the attribute *'ismat,* i.e., freedom from error and the commission of major sin; in Shi'i Muslim belief, the Prophet, his daughter Fatima, and the Twelve Imams.

mufti: a religious scholar qualified to deliver a *fatva.*

mujtahid: a religious scholar qualified to engage in *ijtihad.*

Occultation of the Lord of the Age: the withdrawal from the manifest plane of the Twelfth Imam in the year 260/874; he will return to this plane when God wills.

Reconstruction Jihad: a service organization established after the triumph of the Revolution to perform essential tasks of rural and urban reconstruction.

Sunna: the normative practice of the Prophet Muhammad.

ABOUT THE TRANSLATOR

Hamid Algar was born in 1940 in England and studied Arabic and Persian languages and Islamic Studies at Cambridge University. Since 1965 he has been teaching in the Department of Near Eastern Studies at the University of California, Berkeley, where he is now Professor of Persian and Islamic Studies. Professor Algar has written extensively on the religious history of Iran. Among his published works is *Religion and State in Iran, 1785-1906*. He is currently working on a history of the modern Islamic movement in Iran and a history of one of the major Sufi orders.